YOUR KNOWLEDGE HAS VALUE

- We will publish your bachelor's and master's thesis, essays and papers

- Your own eBook and book - sold worldwide in all relevant shops

- Earn money with each sale

Upload your text at www.GRIN.com and publish for free

Bibliographic information published by the German National Library:

The German National Library lists this publication in the National Bibliography; detailed bibliographic data are available on the Internet at http://dnb.dnb.de .

This book is copyright material and must not be copied, reproduced, transferred, distributed, leased, licensed or publicly performed or used in any way except as specifically permitted in writing by the publishers, as allowed under the terms and conditions under which it was purchased or as strictly permitted by applicable copyright law. Any unauthorized distribution or use of this text may be a direct infringement of the author s and publisher s rights and those responsible may be liable in law accordingly.

Imprint:

Copyright © 2018 GRIN Verlag
Print and binding: Books on Demand GmbH, Norderstedt Germany
ISBN: 9783668758094

This book at GRIN:

https://www.grin.com/document/434723

Hany Fawwaz

The Relation Between the Climate Change, the LGBT Rise, Automation and Economy

GRIN Verlag

GRIN - Your knowledge has value

Since its foundation in 1998, GRIN has specialized in publishing academic texts by students, college teachers and other academics as e-book and printed book. The website www.grin.com is an ideal platform for presenting term papers, final papers, scientific essays, dissertations and specialist books.

Visit us on the internet:

http://www.grin.com/

http://www.facebook.com/grincom

http://www.twitter.com/grin_com

Climate Change+ LGBT Rise+ Automation =Uncommon Relations

Hany Fawwaz   **MAY 2018**

Today It's very common in current world to find tendencies between individuals in every society to express their sexual choices, In this discussion we aren't concerned about the religious or Social debates either LGBT people are right or not, we just tend here to discuss results on economics& societies indicating the climate change role.

Table of Content

Introduction: Defining Relations..2

How to discuss this document?...2

Relation Chain between Climate Change & LGBT Rise.................2

Impacts on societies, Study Case : USA...5

Impacts on Economies*Relation between LGBT Rise & productivity..5

LGBT Rise impact on Industries..6

LGBT Rise & Automation Deployment in Heavy Intensive Industries..6

LGBT Rise Impact on Other Industries...7

Conclusion..8

References 9

About author 10

Introduction: Defining Relations

Different studies suggest that the change in sexual identity is formed in the early life of the child where familial problems can be responsible for it, causes such as the absence of father or man role in the family can do ,Other causes can be hormonal or external environmental like the social stigma or even depressive disorders can go for same results in some personalities (1) .

The key factor is the No believe by person in his current psychological module which tends latterly to developed to be personal and sexual refusal for identity.

Some other undisclosed causes that experts consider is the climate change where it has an indirect influence on the behavior of individuals, Experts say that climate change impacts can prevail to different unexpected aspects like mental health , physiological disorders, violence, HIV Increase and others can lead to change in sexual behavior in direct or indirect way (2) , This means that such acquired new changes in personalities (violence\depressed or changed sexual identities can negatively effect the productivity in societies yield to climate change and lgbt rise.

In this paper we tend to discuss the most undisclosed debates about individual sexuality expression and relation to climate change ,automation and the macro economy drawing opinions based on actual facts (Hany.T.Fawwaz)

How to discuss this document?

Author : Hany Tarek Fawwaz

Start Writing Date 23 feb 2018   Publication Date : 25 MAY 2018

Relation Chain between Climate change & LGBT Rise

1st loop : Climate Change relation to familial violence and children identities

Experts say climate change impacts make people more violent ,when they exposed to high temperatures ,the productivity will be low and potential social losses can occurs for individuals , also loss of jobs can develop depression & to trigger familial violence & aggressive behaviors towards children &women in families, the relation is clear and deepened by time as climate changes increases, (2) if people are very depressed they aren't likely going to be productive or work effectively , they are likely to destructive behaviors like overeating and substances abuse , unless these risky behaviors controlled or medically helped , the society is to going to see impacts .

The familial violence can affect the children personalities and their developed sexual identities which were considered by several studies were" C.G.N " or childhood gender nonconformity is believed to be the largest predictor of homosexuality in adult hood

C.G.N Is considering interests , toys favour and feelings of children to opposite or same sex ,as example a male child may prefers dolls than cars or baby girl prefer the opposite (3) .

The interesting is , researchers found that C.G.N may be results of different causes including the parental care !

Researchers have provided evidences that gay males report having problems with their parents like less care, love and more rejection and close relation to their mothers ,indicating that familial role is very important to the male child, if father's love and care is lost the male child will look for alternative males in family to see the missed caregiver (sex abuses cases) or get close to his mother to get the missed love(this connection can motivate hormone imbalance or the already genetics if any in the child to shift to homosexuality or refusing his own gender identity , this can be an illustration for more sissy boys appearance today .

2nd Loop : Climate change relation to Mental Health

In a report published by cnn in may 2017 , climate change was accused to provide suitable climate for violence and many other mental problems like suicide accidents reported thanks to loss of crops (droughts) or floods(2) .

c.n.n cited by a study made by james rubin ,a psychologist at king college, London about the psychological impacts of floods of people directly & indirectly affected , results show that climate changes can lead farmers ,traders and other associated people to suffer worry , anxiety , aggressive tendencies including suicide for those who can't pass and cope , these threats can lead the exposed persons to the worse like developing severe depression ,tension disorders ,PTSD and other unpleasant mental conditions on the state of mind of millions around our world(4) . Another form of impacts from climate change is the sea level rise and land change in which forced migrants appeared in different areas in the world and they are likely to have pstd with their bad memories of losing properties , dead family members in floods and other similar disasters they faced in their homes(2).

3rd loop : Climate Change& Sexual Behavior

The hormonal imbalance is another key reason for sexuality behavior change especially in manhood gender where the feminine male is almost suffering from high estrogen which usually comes from 3 routes : First is the blocked testosterone hormone converted to estrogen: this is supported by the stress and negativity the male is living in which freely release cortisol (5)at high rate simulating the suitable environment to more estrogen release or blocking testosterone ,

Second is from mental health problems steamed from negative Nutrition style or Mental disorders or else causes like stressful living conditions as example the depressed person has high level of estrogen than normal in comparison to other individual of the same gender (6)(5),

Third route is a blend of the two going for long term where the male became with an estrogenic personality and is dominated by estrogen on the long run where the high female hormone is able to transform the male brain to be feminine Meaning ; to act as an opposite gender , Thinking ,actions, interests and body languages are in adaption to the opposite life style the brain wants to be , scientists found similar parts of the the brain of homosexual men with the same structure of women brain.

The interesting is : It is believed that there is a link between climate change and sexuality of manhood like testosterone blocking action causing low sex drive and other problems in men(7) this mean that as long the climate change continues the heterosexual males are exposed to sexual problem on long run and the homosexual are highly motivated to go for more change in sexual behavior especially those with historical family record of similar cases.

Linkage between loops to make the chain !

The problems in societies like economic and political instability reflect on the life of citizens making them more vulnerable for several personality changes like depression\stress\ violence and all other mental disorders including change in sexual behaviors for both hetro and homo persons as a logical conclusion link between poor sexual life with a low sex drive when people live under stress & continuous challenges.

changes are put in to action in absence of religions which is the mark of most living societies ,with more problems , the individuals lose the guide, one physiological solution the mind adopts in facing problems is to try to protect it self by creating a shed, it can be an adaptive choice to addict drug or violent behavior or certain sexual change or else according to each personality(8)(9) .

all these are factors should be considered when we draw a present and future conclusion about the climate change impact on individual in a given community like the lgbt community which is on rise

Impacts on societies

Study case : USA

In studies conducted by pew research center in feb2018 (10), it was believed that there are links between the unstability of economic conditions and the familial problems derived from non constant financial stability,the center conclude that most single persons prefer goo for long stay with no marriage , and median age for people at first marriage reached 25.5 years \men and 27 \women with declension in marriage rates to divorce rates, Also 54% of previously married women refused to for next marriage and those who got marriage did it on a base of educational gap between the wife and husband, this means more feminine role in the family and imperfect marriage relations that can can impress the children's lives and stability of the families in that given society .

The center gave an interest for lgbt society in us where same sex marriage increased by 61% between couples with public support at 54% in 2017 to 37% in previous year, this means a favour expected increase in such marriage and more members join the lgbt club and more cost on the macro economy of usa(11) .

Impacts on Economies

Relation between LGBT Rise & productivity

The next important question is : what is the relation of sexuality change to the productivity ?

Most lgbt try accept their new life, to accept change ,is it not that easy where they almost face several refusal degrees in there societies, they find discriminations in sreets, in work place and other aspects ,they can't live as free and normal, in studies carried out on LGBT students in united states and Thailand(12) , between 1\2 :2\3 of students are bullied at schools and 1\3 escape from harassment ending with 40% of them to be homeless queers in streets of US compared to 10% of normal young youth in the American nation

Some few could face & overcome , the notable success for some of them is in involvement into charitable works and careers with no audience interactions like soft ware engineering , surely it is a positive thinking and actions but we can't put in the numerical count of productivity , meaning they are not real productive assets as workers ,study conducted for the world bank on 2015 concluded that the discrimination to LGBT community in india could cost the economy up to 32 billions dollars yearly , reason is ,at the macro level , more lgbt with no right education or jobs means more loss to economy in jobs and productivity .

LGBT Rise impact on Industries

Sexual behavior subjects to changes in human life for several times ,reasons vary from person to person to become attracted for the same or opposite gender , The increased numbers of lgbt persons creates a shift towards feminism trends ,After our previous discussions we have enough reasons now to forecast continuous raise of lgbt peoplehood around the globe, numbers still not précised due to social and several causes but the change is already happening and seen at different fields in our new life including commercial trends related to feminism products !

LGBT Rise & Automation Deployment in Heavy Intensive Industries

Heavy Intensive Industries

Also it is hard for gay males to work in heavy intensive industries where such industry needs muscles works which is the contradictive concept of homosexuality derived from their inner identities refuse and active look toward the opposite feminist gender. That makes a shortage and loss in employment in such industries , continuous efforts are exerted to replace workers by automation which still expensive to use on general way (13) .

LGBT Involvement in armies

Also it is important to know that most lgbt individuals are peaceful persons where the living concept is the try to claim their rights and protections in civil peasful actions avoiding disputes in society , so when they go for an empowerment in army entities their violence behavior is almost very low compared to normal soldiers or lesbian or normal women involved in same devices (14).

This can be a serious problem on long run in the structures of armies in most developed countries compared to the armies of third world nations where liberalized acts like lgbt calls are not llegal to represent in army like large presentation found in us or Israel defense army .

Western governments are trying to decrease depending on humans in wars(15)(16) , and deploy automation and apply deep learning algorithms to keep the superiority but not for long because the suspecting dilemma asks who will win ,? the machine or human ? can AI Robot win over a real fighter in actual land fields?

The lgbt rises involvement in western armies can be considered a weakness point in the by which western government try to cover by continuous increasing investment in automation supported by mass destructive weapons , but what will happen if this machine damaged ?what if the enemy develop a destructive systems? Answer is war is a war since the start of human kind, weaker can't flee if his sheds has got damaged , men muscles will be a measure .

LGBT Rise Impact on Other Industries

Fashion Industry

Most lgbt individuals are interested in fashions as a feminine sign plus they tend to be loyal for brands which go for supporting lgbt rights. Related studies found that lgbt individuals spend more on shopping ,Same sex couples spends 25% more than average household on any given shopping trip .

According to witeck-combs communications inc , the purchasing power for lgbt members at 2012 was estimated by 2 trilions dollars & members loyal to the companies that supports their rights,they keep buying from certain brands & as a result of that ,several big companies saw lgbt people important and loyal consumers and domestic partner for long term of success(17) (18).

Air Industry

According to researches analyzing the us consumers behavior, it was found that lgbt individuals are recognized as large traveling consumers for annual and multi annual trips spending 65 bilions on travel totaling 10% of the us travel markets ,

American air line saw an advantage from lgbt people making special targeting marketing for them(19).

Wine industry

according to community marketing inc , 90% of lesbian and 88% of gay men are dining out with friends in bars or nigh clubs with high consuming behavior for beverages (20) .

Children care related industries :

Lgbt members share the concept of making a family as normal couples ,they tend to adapt less children than heterosexual partners(10) .

Sex Toys Industry :

Accodring to susan colvin the co founder of CALEXOTICS , this industry is continuing to develop huge sales standing at 15bilions $ in 2016 with projection that it will surpass 50$ by 2020 ,where the industry worths billions .

According to inverse.com , the LGBT rise has not only created civil rights for individuals but also has created new market for in such fast cash industry where entrepreneurs are racing to gain the market shares .

According to market research group statistic brain , the sex toy sales were estimated by 15billions $ in 2014 and can reach 52 billions $ by 2020 indicating there are plenty of reasons link lgbt buyers to sales revenues where this opinion is supported by Sarah Sloane ,the sexuality and relationship educator and Ex manager of sex toy shop pleasure chest ,were she concluded that several marketing campaigns have been and currently deriven by people who are lgbt -identified both in terms of manufacturers and in terms of people who are doing the product imagination & creation of it (21)(22) .

Music industries

sales records and concerts :

Lgbt community members do notable sales for concerts and records in music industry like products of lady gaga , kylie minogue (23)

Market research and family changes :

According to analysis of a (24) gallup survey shows detailed estimation during 202 :2014 for area with high lgbt density in usa ,result was for san Francisco , CA , then Portland's, and the marketing strategies in those areas were shifted to match the change in family configuration than usual as one family can have one child with two fathers or mothers .

Conclusion

-Climate change is a deep serious topic with countless impacts on our life, governments should take real corrective action to stop and save the possible , Every change takes place is a loop for another change.

-Individualism can indirectly affect the society and economy.

-Mental health and psychology of citizens need to be re evaluated and get more interest to avoid future negative impacts can affect the economy , a possible investment in such fields can be considered,(Scientific plan to use machine learning and AI in solving social problems and mental health improvement was developed by the author in arabic in may 2018).

References

1-www.ncbi.nlm.nih.gov jun 1 2013 Major depression and risky sexual behavior

MARCH 14 2017 How climate change will threaten mental health C.N.N 2-

3-ncbi.nlm.nih.gov by childhood gender nonconformity : A risk indicator for child abuse and posttraumatic stress in youth

4-the impact of climate change on youth depressions and mental health : thetalent.com by H. majeed

How climate change affects your community's mental health : pathpositive.org april 20 2017

5- nyu.edu : Researcher identify stress hormone differene among gay men?

6-ncbi.nlm.nih.gov : Effects of seasonal differences in testosterone and cortisol levels

7-C.N.N Nov 6 2015 Climate change is killing our sex drive; Study says

8-Religious views among gays , bisexual ,lesbians,transgender people: huffpost ; jun 14 2013

9-l'egypte envisage d'interdire l'atheime car une telle absence de religion : dec 25 2017 codesdegay.com

10-pweresearch center feb 13 \2018 : 8 Facts about love andmarriage in America

11-people-press.org 26\6\2017 : support for same sex marriage grows even among groups that had been skeptical

12-world economic forum.org : jan5\2016 charles Radcliffe chief of the global issues ,united nations human rights office

(13) LGBT Military : Hurdles remain for Lgbt soldiers : Georgia voice may 26 2016

)14) gays in militart : rand.org

15-Robot poised to take over wide ranhe of military jobs sandiedouniontribune.com: feb 20 2017

16-automationarmy.io

17-PDF Site resources ,Worldbank : globalization impacts on gender equality

18-the simple reason why so many business support LGBT rights : weforume.org jan 14 2017

19-American airlines-Marketing the rainbow.info

20-PDF : LGBT Market insights-EXPERIAN

21-inverse.com: jan 23 2017

22-forbes jul15 2016 How the niche sex toy market grew into anunstoppable $15B industry

23-Phoenicx,shane; The 2010 LGBT music un review-Hotspot magazine jan21 2011

24-in US , more adults identifying as LGBT : JAN 11 2017 gallup.com

About Author

Name : Hany Tarek Fawwaz   **Origin** : Egypt

Work : Idea Hamster & Independent Researcher , Translator for English ,Arabic & Spanish .

Some published works for the author :

QATAR'S ISOLATION, IS IT POSSIBLE TO END THE QATARI DREAM ? -

UN Biased COMMERCIAL RESEARCH DISCUSSING THE DIPLOMATIC CRISIS OF THE EMIRATE SPANISH\ENGLISH &ARABIC 2017

CLIAMTE CHANGE &INTERNATIONAL TRADE; ALETRS &CHANCES - 2017:2018

-FLYASH IMPACTS ON EGYPTIAN ENVIRONMENT 2014 RETRIVED 2017

YOUR KNOWLEDGE HAS VALUE

- We will publish your bachelor's and master's thesis, essays and papers

- Your own eBook and book - sold worldwide in all relevant shops

- Earn money with each sale

Upload your text at www.GRIN.com and publish for free